J B Pas $ 13.95   OF
Newfield, Marcia.
The life of Louis Pasteur /

885523

PRESS
CARD
HERE

PIONEERS IN HEALTH AND MEDICINE

The Life of
Louis Pasteur

PIONEERS IN HEALTH AND MEDICINE

The Life of
Louis Pasteur

Marcia Newfield
Illustrated by Antonio Castro

Twenty-First Century Books

A Division of Henry Holt and Co., Inc.

Frederick, Maryland

Published by
Twenty-First Century Books
A Division of Henry Holt and Co., Inc.
38 South Market Street
Frederick, Maryland 21701

Text Copyright © 1992
Twenty-First Century Books
A Division of Henry Holt and Co., Inc.

Illustrations Copyright © 1992
Twenty-First Century Books
A Division of Henry Holt and Co., Inc.

Printed in Mexico

10 9 8 7 6 5 4 3 2 1

Library of Congress Cataloging in Publication Data
Newfield, Marcia
The Life of Louis Pasteur
Illustrated by Antonio Castro
(A Pioneers in Health and Medicine Book)
Includes index and bibliographical references.
Summary: The life and work of the noted French scientist
whose discoveries, including a rabies vaccine and the process
of pasteurization, had important practical applications in both
medicine and industry.
1. Pasteur, Louis, 1822-1895—Juvenile literature. 2. Scientists—
France—Biography—Juvenile literature. 3. Microbiologists—
France—Biography—Juvenile literature. [1. Pasteur, Louis,
1822-1895. 2. Scientists.]
I. Castro, Antonio, 1941— ill. II. Title. III. Series: Pioneers in
Health and Medicine.
Q143.P2N38 1991 509.2—dc20 [B] 91-28895 CIP AC
ISBN 0-941477-67-3

Contents

1

"Onward!"

Joseph Meister looked at the unfamiliar room. He stared at the shelves piled high with strange, shiny instruments. "Will they be used on me?" he thought. Joseph shifted nervously in his chair. He felt the painful dog bites scrape against his bandages. He didn't know if he could bear another operation.

Joseph was only nine years old.

In a corner of the room stood an elderly, bearded man. He was Louis Pasteur, the most famous scientist in France. Pasteur shared the young boy's pain and worry. His eyes were edged with deep circles. Louis Pasteur knew the dangers that Joseph faced.

Two days before, on July 4, 1885, Joseph had been attacked by a dog with rabies, a disease that strikes the nervous system. Without treatment, it was almost certain that Joseph would be dead within weeks.

Joseph would not be the first person to die from rabies. In 1885, there was no proven cure for this disease. The doctor in Joseph's small town did the best that he could. Desperate to help the injured boy, he tried to burn away the rabies by pouring a harsh acid on Joseph's open wounds. There was little chance that this painful treatment would work, however.

There was one person who might be able to save Joseph's life. Joseph's doctor had heard about a new rabies treatment, a treatment that had not yet been tested on humans. He told Joseph's mother that the boy's only hope for recovery was hundreds of miles away, in Paris—in the laboratory of Louis Pasteur.

Joseph and his mother traveled by stagecoach to Paris, arriving on the morning of July 6. They went directly to Pasteur's laboratory. The scientist listened carefully to the young boy's story.

Then, he quickly summoned two doctors for their advice. They told Pasteur that the boy would almost surely die from the infection. With each passing hour, the disease was spreading through Joseph's body. The boy must be given the new rabies treatment at once.

Louis Pasteur had recently developed a way to protect animals from getting rabies. He had injected a weakened dose of rabies into healthy dogs. The dogs didn't show any signs of the disease. Over a period of weeks, Pasteur gave the dogs stronger and stronger doses of rabies. Still, there were no symptoms of the disease! At last, the dogs were able to resist a full-strength dose of rabies. They remained healthy even when they were bitten by other animals who had the rabies disease.

Not everyone was convinced by Pasteur's experiment. Many doctors and scientists simply could not accept the idea that he was putting the rabies infection into animals instead of trying to burn out the disease. They accused Pasteur of trying to kill, not cure, the laboratory animals.

Such criticism weighed heavily on Louis Pasteur. He was certain that this new treatment could prevent people from getting rabies *before* they were bitten. But could it fight the rabies infection *after* it had already entered a person's body?

This was not the only concern. What if the rabies treatment was as harmful as the disease itself? Was there a chance that Joseph could survive the rabies infection—only to be killed by Pasteur's "cure"? Even Pasteur's most trusted assistant thought the treatment was too dangerous.

The great scientist searched his heart for the right course to follow. But there was not much time. At last, Pasteur decided that the new treatment was Joseph's best chance for survival.

It was on the evening of July 6, 1885, that Joseph Meister received his first injection. He was scheduled to receive 11 more shots, each one stronger than the last, over the next 10 days. The results of the treatment would not be known for several weeks.

Pasteur arranged a comfortable place for his new patient to stay. He told Joseph's mother not to worry. But Pasteur was unable to follow his own advice.

Each day, he carefully observed Joseph, watching for the slightest sign of rabies. As the shots became stronger, Pasteur grew more and more nervous. His sleep was disturbed by nightmares.

"Your father had a bad night," Louis Pasteur's wife, Marie, wrote to their children. "He is dreading the last inoculations on the child. And yet there can be no drawing back now!"

Louis Pasteur was not the first scientist to wonder about the cause of diseases like rabies. Nor was he the first person to develop methods to fight disease. But Pasteur's work challenged the scientific beliefs of his time and changed the course of medical research.

For thousands of years, most people thought that disease was caused by forces beyond human control. Disease was considered a punishment sent by angry gods, or it was thought to be the work of evil spirits.

It was only gradually that people began to ask new questions about the cause of disease. They looked for answers inside the human body. Perhaps disease occurred when the parts of the body were somehow "out of balance." And they looked for answers outside the body. Perhaps disease came from "bad air."

Without scientific proof, however, these answers were only guesses. And without a scientific method to examine and test ideas about disease, these guesses were often wrong. People remained almost powerless to prevent or cure disease.

Louis Pasteur changed that. He enabled people to understand the basic cause of disease. He gave people the power to protect life and health.

What made him such a great scientist?

Pasteur possessed a rare combination of qualities that were perfectly suited for scientific pursuits. His curiosity drove him to explore the secrets of nature, to wonder why and how nature works the way it does. His courage allowed him to ask why, to give voice to his questions, even when such questions challenged long-held beliefs. His imagination led him to ask the right questions, questions that no one had thought to ask before. His determination made him search until he found the correct answers.

But Louis Pasteur was more than a great scientist. His drive to investigate the secrets of nature was only equalled by his desire to share the knowledge that he gained. For Pasteur, the goal of science was to serve the public good. Scientific research was a way to make people's lives safer and healthier.

Louis Pasteur began his career as a teacher. He was bold and captivating in the classroom. Pasteur's motto was "Onward!" and he taught his students to challenge any belief or practice that did not stand up to scientific inquiry.

Pasteur never really stopped being a teacher. He never stopped sharing his enthusiasm for the value of scientific research. During a celebration in honor of his seventieth birthday, Louis Pasteur looked out at a new generation of scientists and gave fitting expression to his lifelong passion:

> As you pursue your careers, say to yourself, "What have I done for my instruction?" And as you gradually advance, "What have I done for my country?" Until the time comes, when you may have the immense happiness of thinking that you have contributed in some way to the progress and good of humanity.

2

The Will to Achieve

Louis Pasteur grew up in the foothills of the Jura Mountains in eastern France. A countryside of wheat fields, vineyards, and wooded hills surrounded Dôle, the small town where Pasteur was born on December 27, 1822.

Pasteur's earliest memories were of the farmlands near Arbois, where his family settled when he was four, and the distant peaks of the mountains. Many years later, Louis Pasteur still remembered when he would "run joyously" along the country roads.

Louis's "little house," as he called it, was located near a bridge that crossed the Cuisance River. A short hike would take Louis and his school friends by the chemist's shop and the blacksmith's forge, on past the town square, and down to the riverbank. Here, Louis enjoyed long summer days of swimming and fishing. Louis admired the way Jules Vercel, his best friend, tossed a fishing net out on the bright and noisy river.

When his young friends went off to trap birds, however, Louis refused to join them. The sight of a wounded bird, he said, was too painful for him.

Louis's father, Jean Pasteur, was a tanner, a person who turns animal hides into leather. The Pasteur house had a tannery yard in the back, where pits had been dug for the preparation of skins. Louis and his friends would make slingshots and other playthings from pieces of scrap leather while they watched Jean Pasteur at work. Louis's father carefully scraped the fresh animal hides and placed them in the deep pits. Jean then covered the hides with layers of oak bark chips and filled each pit with water.

Louis was fascinated by the tanning process and questioned his father about each step. Why, he asked, does it take a year for the hides to turn into leather? What gives the finished leather its deep brown color?

Jean Pasteur knew that the oak chips released a chemical that made the tough hides softer and more flexible. But Louis's father could not explain how or why the process worked. However, even though he didn't know the answers to all of Louis's questions, Jean encouraged his son's curiosity.

As the evening shadows crept through the "little house," Jean helped Louis with his homework. Reading from his favorite history books, Jean shared with Louis inspiring stories of their country's heroes. He never became annoyed with the young boy's constant

interruptions. Though Louis's father hadn't had much schooling, he understood that learning was based on asking questions.

To Louis, Jean Pasteur was a model of hard work. "Dearest father," Louis later wrote, "it is to you that I owe perseverance in daily work." Jean Pasteur would always be Louis's first, and most important, teacher. As Louis's letters reveal, his father's teaching inspired the young boy to reach for greatness:

> *Not only did you have the qualities which go to make a useful life, but also admiration for great men and great things. To look upward, to learn to the utmost, to seek to rise even higher—such was your teaching.*

Louis's favorite hobby as a boy was drawing and painting. He had a special talent for observation and unusual attention to detail. Louis often pestered his parents and three sisters to sit for their portraits.

Before starting, young Louis studied his models closely. He observed their posture and movement; he noticed what emotions were revealed in their faces. When Louis drew his portraits, he tried not only to sketch what people looked like, but to capture their moods and personalities as well.

When he was 13, Louis sketched a portrait of his mother, Jeanne, in a white bonnet and blue and green checkered shawl. The pastel sketch struck everyone with the way it managed to capture the determined character of Louis's mother.

Years later, Louis again captured the strong spirit of Jeanne Pasteur, this time in one of the many letters he wrote to her. "Your enthusiasm, my brave-hearted mother, you have instilled into me," he said.

The daughter of one of the region's old families, Jeanne Pasteur also shared with Louis a love of one's country and its heroes. "If I have always associated the greatness of science with the greatness of France," Louis observed to his mother, "it is because you have inspired those feelings."

In his early years at school, Louis was not an out-standing student. He finished his assignments more slowly than his classmates and sometimes seemed to be daydreaming. But the truth was just the opposite. Louis Pasteur was a very intent and thorough student. He checked and rechecked each answer before raising his hand. He refused to turn in a test until he was satisfied that each answer was correct. Louis Pasteur simply refused to be wrong.

As Louis progressed in school, his teachers began to see that he had his own way of asking questions and solving problems. He began to win praise for his patient and steady work habits. Monsieur Romanet, the headmaster of Louis's secondary school (or high school), urged Louis to attend college and become a teacher. He spoke to Jean Pasteur, too.

At that time, children of working-class families rarely went to college. Most young men joined their family's trade. This was the path Jean Pasteur had followed: his father and grandfather had been tanners. The Pasteurs took pride in their work and might well have expected Louis to carry on this family tradition.

But Jean and Jeanne Pasteur had other plans for their son. They wanted more for Louis than the back-breaking life of a tanner. His parents agreed that a teaching career was the proper path for Louis, and they saved money to send him to a boarding school in Paris for the last two years of secondary school.

At the boarding school, Louis would prepare to take the entrance examination to the Ecole Normale Supérieure, a teacher's college that trained students to become professors of science, history, literature, or the arts. Only a handful of students were ever accepted. With the prospect of such a future before him, Louis was determined to study even harder.

The fall of 1838 brought cold rains to the French countryside. Louis Pasteur was 15 years old and leaving home for the first time. On a wet October day, he and his friend Jules, who was also going to school in Paris, boarded a stagecoach for the long journey. The familiar sights of Arbois were soon lost to these two young travelers.

Nothing could have prepared Louis and Jules for Paris, one of the world's busiest cities, and Louis soon found out that the thriving capital of France was not the place for him. He could not adjust to the crowded buildings or the bustling streets.

Even though Monsieur Barbet, the headmaster of his new school, was very kind, Louis was too home-sick to concentrate on his work. "If only I could smell a whiff of the tannery yard," he said to Jules, "I feel I should be cured." Three weeks after Louis arrived in Paris, Jean Pasteur, concerned about his son, appeared at the school. "I have come to fetch you," he said.

Back home, Louis Pasteur returned to the Arbois high school. In his spare time, he continued his pastel drawings. Before long, Louis's paintings had formed a masterful portrait gallery of friends and family. He even painted the mayor of Arbois, capturing in his smiling face and strong, blue eyes the outward signs of small-town pride and dignity.

There is no record of Louis's feelings about his failure to adjust to Paris. But it is clear that he hadn't given up his goal of attending the Ecole Normale. The next year, Louis asked his parents for permission to attend a preparatory school in Besançon, located only 25 miles from Arbois.

The Pasteurs were hesitant, concerned that Louis would become homesick again. But he assured them that whenever he felt uneasy or lonely, he would visit home. Louis pointed out that he could see his father when Jean Pasteur traveled to Besançon on business.

Louis couldn't smell a whiff of the tannery at the new school, but he was happy nonetheless. He took classes in drawing and performed well in history and geography. But his best subjects were the sciences.

It was in Besançon that Louis Pasteur discovered how much he enjoyed concentrating on an experiment and analyzing the results. His personality and talents matched the demands of scientific studies. And the sciences, Louis began to realize, could help him find answers to the many questions of his youth.

"Armed with science," an excited Louis wrote his parents, "one can rise above all one's fellows."

Louis became so engrossed in science, in fact, that he put aside most of his other interests. His mind was set on college. For a young man, Louis had a remarkable sense of purpose and determination. His letters home reveal the strength of his emerging character:

> *To will is a great thing, for Action and Work usually follow Will and almost always Work is followed by success. These three things—Will, Work, Success—fill human existence. Will opens the door to success both brilliant and happy; Work passes these doors, and at the end of the journey, Success comes to crown one's efforts. And so, if your resolution is firm, your task, be it what it may, is already begun; you have but to walk forward, it will achieve itself.*

People continued to respond favorably to Louis's drawings. He was even nicknamed "the artist." But Louis would not allow himself to be distracted. When one of his portraits was selected for a local art exhibit, he wrote to his parents, "All this does not lead to the Ecole Normale."

In his second year at Besançon, Louis was chosen to be an assistant teacher. He enjoyed helping other students and began to think that he would make a good teacher. In return for his work, Louis was given free meals, a small salary, and, best of all for such a serious student, his own room.

He now had the privacy he needed to concentrate on his studies. "I have more time for myself," Louis wrote. He closed one of his many letters home with the announcement that "I am beginning to hope that by working as I do, and shall continue to do, I may be received with a good rank at the Ecole."

In August 1842, Louis Pasteur graduated from the Besançon school with honors in physics, mathematics, and Latin. He also received the school's first prize for drawing. Soon after graduation, he took the entrance tests in science for the Ecole Normale.

Only 22 students from across the country were accepted for admission. Louis was fifteenth on the list.

Louis was deeply troubled by his performance. He felt that he had not done his best. Certain that he could improve his scores if he concentrated more on his studies, Louis decided to give up drawing. For the rest of his life, the only drawings he did were related to his scientific experiments. And Louis declined the Ecole Normale's offer of admission, a most unusual thing to do. Instead, he enrolled in the Lycée Saint-Louis, a college preparatory school in Paris.

Now, at age 19, Louis Pasteur was perfectly at home in the city. "I am not homesick this time," he told his relieved parents. Working harder than ever, Louis had very little time to be homesick. He attended classes every day and spent free hours in the library. Each morning, he gave private science lessons to help pay for his schooling.

When friends voiced their concern that he was overworking, Louis wrote, "Do not be anxious about my health and work. I need hardly get up till 5:45 [in the morning]. You see, it's not very early."

Louis took the entrance exams a second time in 1843, placing fourth. Now satisfied that he had done his best, Louis Pasteur entered the science department of the Ecole Normale. He was going to study physics and chemistry. One day, he would be a teacher.

3

A Tale of
Two Discoveries

Paris offered a world of opportunity to a young science student. The buildings near the Ecole Normale housed lecture halls and laboratories. Students jostled one another for the best seats at lectures or scientific demonstrations. Like many eager students of the time, Louis Pasteur felt the strong, almost magical power of scientific discovery.

Of special interest to Pasteur were the lectures by the famous chemist Jean-Baptiste Dumas. "You cannot imagine," he said, "what a crowd of people come to these lectures. The room is immense, and always quite full. We have to be there half an hour before the time to get a good place, as you would in a theater."

Pasteur dreamed of becoming a science teacher, but he knew that working, not wishing, was the way

to achieve this. Each long day of classes ended with Pasteur huddled before the stove, prepared for a long night of studying: first chemistry, then mathematics, and then physics.

Pasteur was responsible for tutoring students and teaching classes. He brought to this work an intense desire, as he wrote, "to perfect myself." To his friend Charles Chappuis, Pasteur described his goals: "Those of us who are to become professors must make the art of teaching our chief concern." Pasteur was proud to report that he had presented a "good" physics lesson. "The one in chemistry," he added, "was perfect."

Pasteur followed this rigorous work schedule for three years. He could barely make time to take a walk with his friend Chappuis. When they did walk along the cobblestone streets, the topic of their conversation was always the same: the research of scientists like Dumas; the noted physicist, Jean-Baptiste Biot; or the chemist, Antoine-Jérôme Balard.

Impatient to make his mark among such names, Pasteur wished he had started his scientific education at an even younger age.

In 1845, Louis Pasteur's hard work brought him the degree he had so single-mindedly pursued. Of the 14 people who took the test to become a professor, Pasteur was one of only four who passed. "Will make an excellent professor," his teachers wrote on his final report. However, before Pasteur could find out if they were correct, he accepted a position in the laboratory of Monsieur Balard. His research there would enable Pasteur to work toward the more advanced Doctor of Science degree.

As his area of research, Louis Pasteur chose to study the nature of crystals, tiny fragments of matter that form the structure of many other substances. It was not surprising that Pasteur picked such a subject. The artist in him was attracted to the beauty of their shapes, like the snowflakes that fell on the streets of Paris. And to the scientist, crystals posed a fascinating mystery, a problem to which Louis Pasteur could not help but be drawn.

At the turn of the nineteenth century, Monsieur Biot had discovered that crystals have the ability to bend a beam of light that passes through them. This ability to bend light is called "optical activity." Biot observed that certain crystals rotate light to the right while others rotate a beam of light to the left.

Other scientists who studied crystals noted that the shape of a crystal seemed to determine the direction of its optical activity. Some crystals were shaped in a right-handed way and bent light in that direction. Crystals that were shaped in a left-handed way bent light to the left.

Pasteur understood this as he began to study two kinds of crystals that commonly formed in the large, wooden kegs used to make wine. One of these crystals was tartaric acid; the other was called paratartaric, or racemic, acid.

A German chemist, Eilhardt Mitscherlich, was the first to observe these crystals. He noted "some very curious findings" about them. Mitscherlich saw that these crystals have "the same crystal shape." Yet he found that they did not have the same kind of optical activity. Tartaric acid crystals bend light, as might be expected, but crystals of racemic acid have no effect on light at all.

It didn't make sense. If the crystals were the same shape, they should have the same effect on light. If crystals showed evidence of different optical activity, they should have different shapes. It certainly didn't make sense to Pasteur, a young researcher at the very start of his scientific career.

In his own account of these years, Pasteur noted that he "meditated for a long time" upon this problem. "I couldn't understand," he recalled, "that two substances could be as similar as claimed by Mitscherlich without being completely identical."

To solve this riddle, Louis Pasteur employed the procedure of analysis and discovery called the scientific method. He first identified the problem and then stated it as a question: why would crystals with the same shape have different kinds of optical activity?

Next, Pasteur formed a hypothesis, a reasonable explanation for the problem. Pasteur's hypothesis was simple. He proposed that tartaric and racemic acids actually had different shapes.

It was a bold suggestion, one that contradicted the judgment of a well-known and respected scientist. But Pasteur sensed that Mitscherlich was wrong. He must have missed something. The crystals *had* to have different shapes, Pasteur believed.

Pasteur put his hypothesis to the test. He spent long hours at his microscope, observing the crystals. He built instruments for measuring the angles of light that passed through them. He sketched the crystals and even prepared wooden models of their shapes. He checked and rechecked his findings against those obtained by other scientists.

Pasteur spent so much time on the problem of crystals, in fact, that his friends began to refer to him as a "laboratory pillar."

And one day, Louis Pasteur saw something he had never seen before—something no one had ever seen before. Pasteur noticed that on some crystals of racemic acid, a facet, or surface section, was turned to the right. At once, he saw that on other racemic acid crystals, the same facet was turned to the left.

When Pasteur put right-faceted crystals together, they rotated a beam of light to the right. Left-faceted crystals rotated the light to the left. And when Pasteur made a solution containing both crystals, the crystal solution had no effect on light at all.

The two kinds of racemic acid crystals cancelled each other out. This was the reason that racemic acid seemed to lack optical activity.

"Suddenly," Pasteur later wrote, "I was seized by a great emotion." He rushed out of the laboratory and embraced a chemistry assistant. "I have just made a great discovery," he exclaimed. "I am so happy I am shaking all over."

The young scientist had been right. The different crystals *did* have different shapes. His discovery was soon the talk of Paris's most famous scientists—from Balard, to Dumas, to a very skeptical Biot. "Are you quite sure?" the elder scientist asked his colleagues. "I should like to investigate that young man's results."

Pasteur repeated his tests. This time, Biot himself even prepared the solutions. The elder scientist saw the light bend exactly as Pasteur had predicted.

Pasteur would always remember Biot's response:

> *The illustrious old man, who was visibly moved, seized me by the hand, and said, "My dear son, I have loved science so deeply that this stirs my heart."*

Pasteur's work was much praised in the scientific circles of Paris. His happiness was marred only by the sudden death of his mother. "She succumbed in a few hours," he told his friend Chappuis. "When I reached home, she had already left us."

Jeanne Pasteur did not die, however, before she could enjoy her son's success. "How fortunate I am, having a child able to raise himself to such a position as yours," she wrote to Louis shortly before her death.

A new phase of Louis Pasteur's career began in January 1849, when he took the position of Professor of Chemistry at the University of Strasbourg. Pasteur was given a laboratory—a poorly equipped one, as most were at that time—and welcomed as a lecturer. He planned to spend his time teaching and continuing his research on crystals.

But he quickly discovered that plans have a way of being unexpectedly changed.

Soon after his arrival at Strasbourg, Pasteur was invited to dinner at the home of the university rector, Monsieur Laurent. There he met Marie Laurent, the rector's pretty, dark-haired daughter. It was, for Louis Pasteur, love at first sight.

According to the customs of the day, Pasteur was not permitted to court Marie before he obtained the approval of her parents. Only two weeks after taking his new position, Pasteur wrote a letter to Monsieur Laurent. He explained that although his family was not poor, he had "long ago decided to hand over" his share of the inheritance to his sisters.

"I have therefore absolutely no fortune," Pasteur said. "My only means are good health, some courage, and my position at the university."

Pasteur expressed himself with similar modesty to Madame Laurent, Marie's mother:

> *I am afraid that Mademoiselle Marie may be influenced by early impressions unfavorable to me. There is nothing in me to attract a young girl's fancy. But my recollections tell me that those who have known me very well have loved me very much.*

When he received permission to write to Marie, Pasteur discovered that the confidence he found in the laboratory left him when his thoughts turned to love. He was afraid that Marie would reject him.

"All I ask of you," Pasteur implored the 22-year-old Marie, "is not to judge me too hastily. You might be mistaken. Time will show that beneath a cold and timid exterior, which may displease you, there beats a heart full of affection for you."

The thought of being rejected was too much for the lovesick young scientist. He wrote Marie again: "I have not cried so much since the death of my mother. I woke up suddenly with the thought that you did not love me and immediately started to cry."

Pasteur even found himself unable to concentrate on his work. "My work no longer means anything to me," he told Marie. "I, who so much loved my crystals. I, who used to wish in the evening that the night be shorter to come back sooner to my studies."

Fortunately for Pasteur and the future of science, Marie accepted Louis's proposal of marriage, and she turned out to be the perfect wife for him. Dr. Emile Roux, Pasteur's associate for over 20 years, described the kind of spouse Louis Pasteur had found:

From the first days of their common life, Madame Pasteur understood what kind of man she had married; she did everything to protect him from the difficulties of life, taking onto herself the worries of the home, that he might retain the full freedom of his mind for his investigations.

Their marriage, as Emile Roux described it, was a true partnership:

Madame Pasteur loved her husband to the extent of understanding his studies. During the evening, she wrote under his dictation, calling for explanations, for she took a genuine interest in crystalline structures. She had become aware that ideas become clearer by being explained to others, and that nothing is more conducive to devising new experiments than describing the ones which have just been completed. Madame Pasteur was more than an incomparable companion for her husband, she was his best collaborator.

Louis and Marie Pasteur soon started a family. In the years ahead, Marie gave birth to two daughters,

Jeanne (in 1850) and Cécile (1853), and a son, Jean-Baptiste (1851).

Pasteur continued to study crystals. But he also began to study the optical activity of living things. He was hoping to find the secrets of their behavior, too.

To Chappuis, Pasteur wrote of his new research:

> *I have already told you that I am on the verge of mysteries, and that the veil which covers them is getting thinner and thinner. The nights seem to me to be too long, yet I do not complain, for I prepare my lectures easily, and often have five whole days a week that I can devote to the laboratory. I am often scolded by Madame Pasteur, whom I console by telling her that I shall lead her to posterity.*

4

Wings of Imagination

In September of 1854, France's Minister of Public Education honored Louis Pasteur by appointing him Professor of Chemistry and Dean of Sciences at the University of Lille.

The University of Lille was a new school. It was located in "the richest center of industrial activity in the north of France," the minister reminded Pasteur. "By giving you the direction of it, I show the entire confidence I have placed in you. I am convinced that you will fulfill the hopes which I have founded upon your zeal."

The new university's mission was to meet "the practical needs" of the region. Pasteur's role was to teach college students how to adapt the lessons of the laboratory to the everyday problems facing the area's industries. It was a challenge that Pasteur was eager to accept.

Louis Pasteur disagreed with those scientists who thought that trying to solve practical problems was not a worthwhile use of scientific knowledge. "There are not two different kinds of science," he remarked. "There is science and the application of science. They are linked together as is the fruit to the tree which bears it."

Pasteur made sure that the fruit and the tree were linked together at the University of Lille. At the opening of the university, he spoke about this important connection:

> *Where will you find a young man whose curiosity and interest will not immediately be awakened when you put into his hands a potato, when with that potato he may produce sugar, and with that sugar alcohol? Where is he who will not be happy to tell his family in the evening that he has just been working on the electric telegraph? Such studies are seldom if ever forgotten.*

As dean of the new school, Pasteur encouraged factory workers to attend college classes at night. And he took his students on tours of farms and factories to show them examples of science in action.

Many of these factories were distilleries, where alcohol was produced through the chemical process of fermentation. Fermentation is a natural reaction—the process, for example, by which yeast turns grape juice into wine. But at the time, no one knew what caused these changes, or why. The leading scientists of the period could only say that the process of fermentation was "strange and obscure." The kinds of questions a young Pasteur once asked about the tanning process needed to be asked once again.

One day in the summer of 1856, a Monsieur Bigo, a distillery owner whose son attended the university, paid Pasteur a visit. Bigo complained that something was going wrong with the fermentation process at his distillery. The beet juice was not turning into alcohol; instead, it was producing a sour, gray soup.

Many other alcohol manufacturers, Bigo reported to Pasteur, were having the same trouble. This was bad news for everyone in the region. The industrial alcohol that had been made there for generations was essential to the production of vinegar, perfume, and paint. Many industries were being affected.

Bigo asked Pasteur to take a look at the problem. For the young teacher, this was an opportunity to put the scientific method at the service of industry and country. Beginning that summer, Pasteur made daily trips to Bigo's distillery.

"Louis is now up to his neck in beet juice," Marie Pasteur wrote to Louis's father. It must have surprised and amused the factory workers to see this bearded man scrambling up ladders to peer into the vats of fermenting beet juice.

Pasteur took samples of the beet juice back to his laboratory, where he examined the liquids with his microscope. Other scientists had noticed that microscopic particles of yeast, called ferments, accompany the fermentation process. It was commonly believed that these ferments were nonliving things that helped to start the chemical reactions of fermentation.

Pasteur observed these ferments carefully. In the "good" fermentation, he saw ferments in the shape of little round globes. These he recognized as yeast cells. In the "bad" juice, these globes were outnumbered by other ferments that were shaped like rods.

Pasteur formed hypothesis after hypothesis about these rod-shaped ferments. If the facts did not support one of his theories, it had to be abandoned. "Error," Pasteur wrote next to each disproven hypothesis.

Louis Pasteur spent hours bent over his microscope, staring at the ferments he called "wee germs." (It was only later that they came to be called microbes or microorganisms.) He recalled the work of Charles Cagniard-Latour, a scientist who suggested that yeast cells showed evidence of reproduction "by a sort of budding." Pasteur formed a new hypothesis. If they were able to reproduce, then perhaps these ferments were actually alive. Perhaps they were feeding on the beet-juice sugar and turning it into alcohol.

To test this idea, Pasteur created different sugary liquids for the yeast cells. Through the microscope, he saw the tiny globes bud and divide. The cells were multiplying before his eyes! Pasteur knew that only living things were able to reproduce. Once again, the scientists had been wrong. These ferments, too small to be seen with the naked eye, were living things.

Startled by this discovery, Pasteur searched for "wee germs" in other liquids. He examined milk, a product that spoils quickly. In milk that had turned sour, he found the same kinds of rods he had seen in Bigo's spoiled beet juice. When Pasteur placed some of these new rods in a dish of fresh milk, they quickly multiplied, thus spoiling the milk. These rods were also alive, he concluded.

Louis Pasteur could now make sense of an amazing microscopic struggle. The yeast cells fed on the sugary juice of the beets and enabled the fermentation process to work. But the rod-shaped ferments could overrun the yeast cells and ruin the process.

In 1857, less than two years after he started his studies on beet juice, Pasteur published his report on ferments. It stated that these microscopic globes and rods were living creatures. Some ferments, such as the globes that turned beet juice into alcohol, were helpful; other ferments, like the rods, were harmful.

Using this new information, Pasteur helped Bigo solve his beet juice problem. The key was to find the rods before they soured the beet juice. Pasteur taught the distillery workers to use microscopes to inspect the vats of juice for the rod-shaped ferments. Once the rods appeared, the juice had to be thrown out.

Pasteur's report that fermentation was "a living process caused by microscopic living things" created a storm of scientific interest and controversy. When a statement describing his research was read to members of the Academy of Sciences, the country's leading scientific society, many members refused to accept the new evidence. But such criticism did not stop Pasteur from continuing his research.

That research would have to be carried on elsewhere, however. Pasteur had accepted the position of Director of Scientific Studies at the Ecole Normale, the school from which he had graduated 10 years before. Back in Paris, he confronted the same problems most scientists of his day faced: poorly equipped laboratory space and not enough money. Pasteur used his own money to transform two rooms in the school's attic into a research laboratory.

There, in this tiny space beneath the roof, where the summer sun raised the temperature to 95 degrees, Pasteur continued to work on fermentation. Now, he wanted to find the origin of germs, the microscopic creatures that had such a big impact on people's lives.

At this time, Pasteur's family life was a source of great happiness. His children were thriving. In 1858, Marie-Louise, a fourth child, was born. Marie and the children often visited Louis at work.

But the next year, tragedy struck. Jeanne Pasteur, now nine years old, became ill with typhoid fever. She soon died from the disease.

Louis and Marie were heartbroken. Louis Pasteur wrote to his father:

> *I cannot keep my thoughts from my poor little girl, so good, so happy in her little life. But forgive me for recalling these sad memories. She is happy. Let us think of those who remain and try as much as lies in our power to keep them from the bitterness of this life.*

When he could once again summon the energy for work, Pasteur returned to the question of where germs came from. Many scientists of the era accepted the concept of spontaneous generation—the idea that germs were created spontaneously, or suddenly, from nonliving matter. Ferments, according to this theory, were created directly from the air, from mud, or from rotting food or waste products.

But Pasteur had seen otherwise. He had watched germs multiply under the microscope, and he knew that they did not emerge "out of thin air."

So Pasteur challenged the theory of spontaneous generation and, in doing so, began another storm of scientific controversy.

Pasteur carried out hundreds of experiments to show that germs come from other germs. Germs, he

insisted, are not created by the air. Germs multiply from other germs, Pasteur believed. They are carried through the air on dust particles until they land.

To prove his theory, Pasteur prepared a liquid in which "wee germs" easily grew. Then, he poured the liquid into a flask, or glass bottle, which had a neck shaped like a long "S." (The shape was suggested by Pasteur's old chemistry professor, Monsieur Balard.) Next, Pasteur boiled the liquid to sterilize it, killing any germs that already existed. Boiling also created steam, which forced the air out of the flask.

As the flask cooled, air returned inside it. But the curved neck allowed only clean air to enter. Any dust particles in the air were trapped in the neck of the flask. Since only clean air, not dust, could reach the liquid, the flask remained sterile, or free of germs.

Pasteur tilted the flask. This brought the liquid into contact with dust particles trapped in the neck of the flask. Within a few days, millions of germs formed a thick, gray coating on the surface of the liquid in the flask—proof that the germs had not arisen from the air. Instead, they had been carried through the air and into the flask by the dust particles.

In 1861, Pasteur and his research assistants carried sterilized flasks to the dustiest places they could find: cellars, city streets, and factories. In each location, his assistants carefully broke off the necks of the flasks and exposed the liquid inside to the air. Whenever dust touched the liquid, a cloudy layer of germs soon covered the surface.

But Pasteur wanted further proof. "Imagination should give wings to our thoughts," he wrote, "but we always need decisive experimental proof."

The same year, Pasteur's search for that decisive proof took him to new heights—to the mountains, in fact. He wanted to show that the amount of germs in the air differed from place to place. The cleaner the air, he reasoned, the fewer the germs.

He traveled to Arbois, with 20 flasks, to test the clean air of his youthful home. Only eight of the 20 samples grew germs.

With another 20 flasks of liquid strapped in cases on a donkey's back, he climbed the steep and snowy mountain peaks of the Alps. The cold wind whipped the scientist as he opened the flasks in the mountain air and then quickly sealed them. When he looked at the sealed flasks later, germs had grown in only one of them. He wrote in his notebook, "If all the results are compared that I have obtained until now, it seems to me that it can be affirmed that the dusts suspended in air are the exclusive origin of life in the liquids in the vessels."

However, not all of Pasteur's scientific colleagues were convinced. For years, the controversy continued. But his work steadily gained influence and respect. On December 8, 1862, Pasteur was elected a member of the Academy of Sciences, the highest honor for a French scientist.

It was to the members of the academy, on April 7, 1864, that Pasteur finally demonstrated the results of his mountain experiment. Before a group of scientists, students, celebrities, and politicians, he displayed one of the sealed flasks of mountain air. After three years, the flask was still free of microscopic life.

Once the flask was opened, Pasteur announced, it would fill with germs within days. "Never will the doctrine of spontaneous generation recover from the mortal blow of this simple experiment," he asserted.

It was a triumph for Louis Pasteur. Germs were everywhere, he told the crowd assembled before him. And they come into the world, he announced, from other germs:

> *There is no known circumstance in which microscopic beings come into the world without germs, without parents similar to themselves. Those who affirm it have been duped by illusions, by ill-conducted experiments, by errors that they did not perceive or did not know how to avoid.*

The debate was over, but Louis Pasteur's work with germs was not. He soon identified the specific germs, both helpful and harmful, that cause different kinds of fermentation. He discovered that lactic acid germs change milk into butter and cheese. He found out that yeasts are the germs that help make bread, wine, and beer.

Pasteur also explored new ways to prevent germs from spoiling food. He developed a way to heat food and drinks so that harmful germs were killed, and he went on to design the industrial equipment that was needed to carry out this process.

Pasteur shared his ideas with people all over the world. The process of using heat to destroy germs, still in use today, bears his name—pasteurization.

5

Higher Summits

By 1865, at the age of 42, Pasteur had won the reputation of being a brilliant and inventive scientist. But he was not content to rest on past accomplishments. To him, a scientist was a true explorer, always "moving forward to the discovery of the unknown."

"The scientist is like a traveler," Pasteur wrote, "who reaches higher and higher summits, from which he sees in the distance new countries to explore."

This explorer could hardly have foreseen where his scientific travels would take him next. He certainly would not have expected his old chemistry professor, Monsieur Dumas, to ask him to look into silkworms. It was to Dumas that the French Minister of Agriculture had turned for help. And Dumas turned to his most famous student, Louis Pasteur.

A mysterious disease was killing the silkworms in France. Without silk to make dresses and suits, the French clothing industry was facing ruin.

49

At first, Pasteur didn't think he could be of much help. "Remember, if you please," he wrote to Dumas, "I have never even touched a silkworm." According to one account, Dumas replied, "So much the better. For ideas, you will have only those which shall come to you as a result of your own observations."

Pasteur could not decline what he called such a "pressing invitation." He had, after all, dedicated his genius to the service of his country. Before long, he started to read everything he could about silkworms.

On June 16, 1865, Pasteur left Paris to establish a laboratory in Alais, a town in southern France at the center of the silkworm-growing region. Marie and the children—including the newest addition to the family, two-year-old Camille—joined him.

In Alais, Pasteur learned that a moth lays up to 400 eggs at a time. Silkworms hatch out 10 days later and feed on mulberry leaves. The worms shed their coverings four times before spinning a silken cocoon when they are about six weeks old. Their cocoons are made of silk fibers that may be as long as 3,000 feet.

The breeders dipped each cocoon in hot water to kill the worm before it could turn into a moth and ruin the silken cocoon. The silk fibers left behind were then woven into fabric.

Pasteur began to make his observations of both healthy and sick worms. He was becoming convinced that the silkworms were the victims of a contagious

disease. Using his microscope, he saw globe-shaped organisms on the sick worms.

Pasteur then taught the silkworm breeders how to use a microscope to spot the globules. This should enable the breeders to weed out diseased silkworms, he assumed.

But a new generation of worms turned out to be diseased even though specimens with the suspicious globules had been destroyed. To make matters worse, there were worms that seemed to be suffering from the disease despite the fact that they did not show any sign of the globules. Not one to give up at this lack of success, Louis Pasteur was determined to uncover the secret of the sick silkworms.

For 18 hours a day, he locked himself away, his attention focused on the world under his microscope. At last, Pasteur learned that there were other kinds of germs infecting the silkworms. They were responsible for a second disease that was killing the worms.

Pasteur's discovery was all the more remarkable in that it was made during a period of great personal tragedy. Only nine days after his arrival at Alais, a telegram called him back to Arbois. His father was very sick. By the time Pasteur reached his boyhood home, Jean Pasteur was dead.

From the tannery, Pasteur wrote a sad message to his wife and children: "Dear Marie, dear children, the dear grandfather is no more; we have taken him this morning to his resting place, close to little Jeanne's." Pasteur had hoped "until the last moment" to see his father again, to "embrace him for the last time." But he could only "accompany him to the grave."

Pasteur shared with his family the deep sense of gratitude that he felt toward his father. "For years, I have been his constant care," Pasteur wrote. "I owe everything to him." For Louis Pasteur, success as a scientist was a way of paying back that debt. He took comfort in the fact that "success in my scientific career must have filled him [Jean] with pride and joy."

The Pasteurs soon endured a series of personal losses. In September of 1865, Camille, only two years old, became ill with typhoid fever. She died within a few months. Pasteur took the coffin to Arbois.

Less than 10 months later, 13-year-old Cécile also caught typhoid fever. Louis and Marie watched helplessly as Cécile, too, died from a disease that doctors were powerless to cure.

His work was Pasteur's only escape. "I am now wholly wrapped up in my studies," he wrote to the French Minister of Agriculture, "which alone take my thoughts from my deep sorrow."

Personal sorrow and the stress of constant work must have exhausted Pasteur. On the night of October 19, 1868, he suffered a cerebral hemorrhage, or stroke. A blood vessel in his brain had burst, and Pasteur was near death.

Throughout the night, Marie sat by her husband's bedside. He was partially paralyzed and often unable to speak. There would be other difficult nights ahead as Louis struggled to recover. At times, he regained his speech. He told Marie not to be frightened for him.

To one of the many friends who came to his bedside, Pasteur whispered, "I am sorry to die, I wanted to do much more for my country." That friend refused to hear such talk. "Never fear," he replied, "you will make many more marvelous discoveries."

Louis Pasteur's hypothesis about his death was wrong. Though his body was permanently damaged, he was soon back to the business of making "marvelous discoveries." One week after the stroke, in fact, he dictated a scientific paper about silkworms for the Academy of Sciences. In January of 1869, only three months after his stroke, Louis astonished his wife and associates by insisting on returning to his laboratory in Alais to finish his research on silkworms.

In 1870, Pasteur published a report on silkworms. He explained that microscopic parasites were spreading disease among the silkworms of France. Pasteur showed silkworm breeders how to find and destroy diseased worms and to use only healthy eggs to raise disease-free worms. This method was soon adopted by silkworm growers throughout Europe.

Louis Pasteur had single-handedly saved the silk industry. He was now hailed as a miracle worker. To many people, there seemed to be no problem that he couldn't solve. But he soon faced an obstacle beyond his power to control.

That obstacle was the war that broke out between France and Prussia in 1870, forcing Pasteur to leave Paris, and his research, behind. When he returned to his home at the war's end in 1871, Pasteur was ready to get back to work. "My head is full of wonderful ideas," he said.

But Paris was full of wounded soldiers. Pasteur's old school, the Ecole Normale, had been turned into a hospital. As Pasteur toured the city's medical clinics, he decided to study samples of infected tissues taken from the soldiers' wounds. Under the microscope, he saw the living creatures that he now knew were the cause of diseases.

He became convinced that doctors themselves— working in dirty conditions, rushing from patient to patient without washing their hands, treating the sick with unclean instruments—were spreading the germs that caused so many infections.

Few doctors were ready to accept the idea that they themselves were spreading germs. But Pasteur was convinced. "I am the most hesitating of men," he said, "the most fearful of committing myself, when I lack evidence. But no consideration can keep me from defending what I hold as true when I rely on solid scientific evidence."

In time, Louis Pasteur's tireless round of reports, lectures, and demonstrations convinced many doctors that strict attention to cleanliness, or hygiene, could save lives.

In 1874, Pasteur received support for this theory from an unexpected place. A Scottish surgeon named Joseph Lister wrote a letter to Pasteur explaining how he had read the French scientist's reports on germs. Lister said that by following Pasteur's suggestions, he had found a way to prevent germs from coming into contact with patients during surgical operations.

Lister sprayed a fine mist of carbolic acid over a patient. Carbolic acid is an antiseptic, a substance that kills germs without harming human tissue. As a result of this new practice, fewer wounds became infected after surgical procedures, thus giving patients a better chance of survival.

Often credited with starting the modern age of surgery, Lister made it quite clear that Louis Pasteur had shown him the way. He invited Pasteur to visit his hospital so that the French scientist could see for himself "how largely mankind is being benefited by your labors."

Two years later, Louis learned about the research efforts of another European doctor, a German named Robert Koch. In 1876, Koch had discovered the specific germ that causes anthrax, one of the most contagious, and most feared, diseases of sheep and cattle.

Pasteur immediately realized the importance of this discovery and set out to test Koch's results. He designed a technique for growing the anthrax germ. He then demonstrated that if a healthy farm animal was given even the tiniest drop of blood infected with anthrax, the animal would develop the disease.

Pasteur sensed that he was on the verge of a great discovery. "At no time in my scientific life," he wrote, "have I worked so hard or been so much interested in the results of my researches." The next year he published his conclusions in a report called "The Germ Theory and its Application to Medicine and Surgery." In this report, he asserted that specific germs cause specific contagious diseases.

The culmination of 20 years of research, the germ theory of disease was the first scientific explanation for the spread of contagious diseases. Now, for the first time, epidemics like cholera and smallpox had an identifiable cause. Now, scientists could start finding the germs that killed so many people. At last, there was hope for a victory in the fight against disease.

6

Armed with Science

Louis Pasteur's germ theory opened the door to the dream that someday there might be a way to cure or prevent the spread of contagious diseases. In 1879, however, that dream seemed very far from becoming a reality.

Chicken cholera was sweeping through the barnyards of France. This disease was so deadly, in fact, that it killed 90 out of every 100 chickens it infected. Pasteur began his study of the epidemic by growing cholera germs. He developed a broth that nourished the growth of the germs. Satisfied with his progress, Pasteur left his work to enjoy a rare summer holiday with his family.

Returning to his laboratory, Pasteur found some old dishes of cholera broth. By now, the broth had become dry and crusted. Surely, it must be stale and useless, Pasteur thought. His first reaction was just to throw these old samples away.

He didn't. Instead, Pasteur injected the dried-out broth into several chickens, thinking that the chickens would soon show the signs of cholera.

The next morning, when Pasteur arrived at his laboratory, he went directly to the chicken cages. To his astonishment, the chickens were clucking busily in their cages. The stale cholera broth hadn't hurt them at all.

Pasteur immediately took advantage of such unexpected results. "In the field of experimentation," he used to say, "chance favors only the mind which is prepared." He knew that the stale cholera broth had lost its power to cause disease.

This episode brought to mind the earlier work of Edward Jenner, a British doctor. In 1796, Jenner found a way to prevent the contagious disease smallpox. By giving people a small dose of cowpox, a milder form of smallpox, Jenner was able to protect them from the more serious disease. But he had no idea how or why his treatment worked.

Jenner's success with smallpox gave Pasteur his hypothesis. Perhaps, the French scientist thought, the stale cholera broth acted like Jenner's dose of cowpox. Perhaps a weakened form of cholera could somehow stimulate the body to fight a full-strength appearance of the germs.

Hypothesis in hand, Pasteur set to work. First, he injected a stronger dose of fresh cholera germs into the chickens that had survived the old broth. At the same time, he gave a fresh dose of cholera to a second group of chickens. When he returned to his laboratory the next day, Pasteur observed that the chickens in the second group were very sick, if not already dead. But the chickens who had received the original dose of chicken cholera broth were healthy.

His hypothesis had been right. A weakened form of cholera germs gave the body protection against the disease. (That protection is called immunity.) In some way, the process of using weakened germs helped the body to resist cholera. In honor of Edward Jenner's contribution, Pasteur called this process vaccination, from "vacca," the Latin word for cow.

"Armed with science," Louis Pasteur now began a scientific crusade against contagious disease.

He discovered a way to heat anthrax germs so that they became too weakened to cause the disease, yet remained strong enough to stimulate immunity. He tested his vaccine by injecting it into sheep. When the sheep were injected again, this time with fresh and deadly anthrax germs, they remained healthy.

"Now," said a triumphant Pasteur, "we have a vaccine that can be sent to all parts of the world."

As always, Pasteur wanted to share his research with other scientists. In 1881, he delivered his report on vaccination to the Academy of Sciences. However, his work was again met with criticism and suspicion.

How could a chemist know so much about an animal disease? The editor of *The Veterinary Journal* proposed a public test of Pasteur's anthrax vaccine.

Pasteur at once accepted the challenge. He would work with two different groups of sheep. One group would be vaccinated twice with his anthrax vaccine; the other group would not be vaccinated. Two weeks later, both groups of sheep would be injected with a full-strength dose of anthrax germs. If the vaccinated sheep remained healthy while the others became sick, the vaccine would be proven to be effective.

The anthrax test was scheduled to take place near the town of Melun, south of Paris. Louis Pasteur was so confident that his anthrax vaccine would work as well in the field as it had in the laboratory that he announced the results in advance. "The unvaccinated sheep will all perish," he said. "The vaccinated ones will survive."

The historic anthrax test was carried out in four parts. On May 5, 1881, Pasteur watched as several of his assistants vaccinated a group of 24 sheep with the anthrax vaccine. Twelve days later, the same animals were vaccinated again, with an even stronger vaccine. A second group of animals, the "control group," was left untouched.

On May 31, a crowd of journalists, government officials, doctors, farmers, and veterinarians gathered at the Melun farm as Pasteur's assistants injected a

full dose of deadly anthrax germs into both groups of animals. The observers were to return to the farm two days later to see the results of the test.

For Pasteur, the long wait was almost unbearable. The next day, June 1, his assistants at Melun brought back some discouraging news. They told Pasteur that several of the vaccinated sheep had now developed high fevers. Knowing that fever was one of the first symptoms of anthrax, Pasteur was alarmed.

Throughout the day, Pasteur became increasingly nervous. "What have I let myself in for?" he asked his wife. "I'm finished. There'll be nothing for me to do but retire. A whole lifetime of work will go for nothing. Tomorrow will be a disaster."

But early the next morning, June 2, 1881, Pasteur received a telegram from one of his assistants. He was too nervous to open it. Marie had to read the telegram to him. It read:

Of the 25 unprotected sheep, 18 are already dead, and the others are dying. All the vaccinated sheep are on their feet. A brilliant success!

When Louis Pasteur arrived at the farm that same afternoon, he was greeted with cheers and applause. Here was a way to prevent anthrax—and here was hope that the same protection could be offered against many other contagious diseases—in humans as well as animals.

"Joy reigns in the laboratory and in the house," Louis Pasteur wrote to his daughter and son. "Rejoice, my dear children."

Pasteur had developed a powerful weapon in the fight against disease. It was a remarkable discovery. In fact, the previous 20 years had seen a remarkable series of discoveries.

First, Pasteur proved that fermentation is caused by microscopic germs and that each specific type of fermentation is caused by a specific germ. His work demonstrated how to protect food from spoiling.

Next, Pasteur proved that contagious diseases are caused by germs and that each disease is caused by the action of a specific germ. His work demonstrated how to keep animals safe from contagious disease.

Finally, Pasteur proved that specific germs can be weakened and then used to prevent disease. His work demonstrated how animals could be given immunity from contagious diseases.

It was, indeed, a remarkable series of discoveries. And now his greatest challenge lay ahead.

7

A Torch for the World

"There can be no drawing back now!"

Marie Pasteur wrote to her children as Joseph Meister lay asleep. Her husband had never been one to draw back. Even before the success at Melun, Louis Pasteur had already chosen the disease he wanted to conquer next.

While working on his vaccine for anthrax in the late 1870s, Pasteur had begun to study hydrophobia, more commonly known as rabies. A contagious disease, rabies is passed to people through the bites of infected animals. At the time, rabies was one of the most terrifying diseases known to humanity.

For many people, the image of a rabid dog, foaming at the mouth and attacking any person in its path, was a symbol of the terror and mystery of all disease. Pasteur felt that if he could conquer rabies, he could alert many more people to the life-saving possibilities of his own germ theory of contagious disease.

But the fight against rabies quickly became one of Pasteur's most difficult problems. It would take him five years to develop an effective vaccine.

Pasteur had found the germs that cause chicken cholera and anthrax in the blood of infected animals. Using similar methods, he now hunted for the rabies germ in the blood of dogs and rabbits who had died from the disease.

Yet no matter how hard and no matter how long Pasteur looked through the microscope at the samples of infected blood, he couldn't find the rabies germ. He reasoned that since rabies develops after a bite from an infected animal, the germ must be in the animal's saliva. But he couldn't find it there, either.

What Pasteur couldn't know at that time was that the germ that causes rabies is a virus. Diseases like cholera and anthrax are caused by organisms called bacteria. Scientists could observe these tiny creatures with the aid of a microscope. However, viruses are so much smaller than bacteria that they can only be seen through microscopes far more powerful than the ones available to the scientists of the nineteenth century.

Pasteur turned his attention to the symptoms of rabies. He knew that rabies victims are frightened by bright lights. The slightest noises startle them. Since these symptoms involve the nervous system, Pasteur thought that the brain must be the secret hiding place of the rabies germ.

There was only one sure way for Pasteur to test his hypothesis. He would have to study the brains of living animals infected with rabies. This was the kind of scientific research that Pasteur hated to perform. "I feel the suffering of animals strongly enough never to have taken up hunting or shooting," he noted. "But when we probe the mysteries of life and acquire new truth, the sovereignty of the end carries all before it."

Pasteur's research showed that rabies did, in fact, form in the brain and spinal cord of infected animals. His assistants removed infected brain tissue from one animal and placed it directly in the brain of a healthy animal. Dogs that were treated this way developed rabies very quickly.

So even though Pasteur couldn't see the germs, he had found out where they live and multiply. He had taken the first step toward controlling the disease.

His next step was to find a way to weaken the rabies germs, as he had done with the germs of chicken cholera and anthrax. He instructed his assistants to remove pieces of infected spinal cord tissue from a group of rabbits that had died of rabies. His assistants then sealed the spinal cord in a sterile flask, which contained a chemical to dry out the cord.

When infected tissue that had been dried for 14 days was injected into healthy dogs, it failed to cause rabies. The rabies germs had been weakened enough so that they no longer caused the disease. Now, using dried spinal cord, Louis Pasteur began the search for a rabies treatment.

He vaccinated a dog with infected spinal cord tissue that had been dried for 14 days. The next day, the same dog was vaccinated with spinal cord that had been dried for 13 days. This procedure continued for 12 more days.

Each day, the dose of rabies germs got stronger and stronger. On the last day of the treatment, the dog was vaccinated with infected spinal cord tissue that had been dried for only one day and was therefore very deadly. However, even when it received an injection of this cord, the dog remained free of rabies.

Pasteur had found the rabies vaccine. He tested it further and discovered that because rabies has such a long incubation period, the vaccine would cure dogs even after they were infected. (An incubation period is the time it takes for a germ that has invaded the body to cause the symptoms of disease.) The rabies vaccine prevented the germ from developing during the six-week period of incubation.

Certain that his rabies vaccine worked, Pasteur now wondered how it could best be put to use. At first, he considered vaccinating every dog in France against rabies. But it would be impossible to vaccinate more than 2 million dogs.

Pasteur decided that the rabies vaccine should be used only on animals and people who had already been infected with rabies. Bravely, Pasteur decided to test the vaccine on himself.

"I have not yet dared to treat human beings after bites from rabid dogs," he wrote to a friend. "But the time is not far off, and I am much inclined to begin by inoculating myself with rabies, for I am beginning to feel very sure of my results."

But Louis Pasteur never had to take that chance. The young boy named Joseph Meister would be his test case.

On the morning of July 16, 1885, Joseph received his last vaccination of dried spinal cord. This was the strongest dose yet. The cord had been dried for only one day. Yet even after this full-strength dose, Joseph remained healthy. He never developed rabies.

Joseph recovered completely from his dog bites. Less than a month after his attack, he was sent home to his village.

"Great things are coming to pass," Louis Pasteur proclaimed. The rabies vaccine was, he said, "one of the great medical facts of the century."

The news of Joseph's recovery spread throughout France. A few weeks later, Pasteur received an urgent appeal to save another boy's life. The mayor of a small town in Jura wrote Pasteur a letter about a 15-year-old shepherd, Jean-Baptiste Jupille, who had been bitten by a rabid dog while trying to save his friends. Could Pasteur be of any help?

Pasteur wrote back immediately, saying that his rabies vaccine had been tested on only one person. However, he felt confident that his treatment could help to save Jean-Baptiste's life.

But the boy would have to travel to Paris at once. There was no time to lose. Six days after the attack, Jean-Baptiste received the first of his vaccinations. His life, too, was saved.

People from all across Europe were soon arriving at Pasteur's laboratory, seeking the miraculous rabies vaccine. Within a period of three months, Pasteur had inoculated 353 people.

As he had done so many times before, Pasteur presented the results of his research to the Academy of Sciences. The date was October 26, 1885. Pasteur explained the way his vaccination program worked. He asked his fellow scientists to establish "an institute for rabies vaccination."

When Pasteur finished his report, the secretary of the academy gave his praise to Pasteur's work. "The date of the present meeting," he claimed, "will remain forever memorable in the history of medicine."

8

The Legacy

By October of 1886, more than 2,400 people had received Pasteur's new vaccine. Although only a very few of them died, some of Pasteur's colleagues argued that the vaccine was too dangerous to use. They even accused him of being a murderer.

But in 1888, an independent medical committee tested the rabies vaccine and proved that it was safe. "We believe that the value of Pasteur's discovery," the members wrote, "will be much greater than can be estimated for it shows that it may become possible to avert other diseases besides hydrophobia."

When the Academy of Sciences launched a fund-raising drive to build a research institute, people from all over the world sent in contributions. On November 14, 1888, the Pasteur Institute was opened with Louis Pasteur as its director. One of the most modern scientific facilities in the world, the institute was "devoted to public health."

Having suffered another stroke, Pasteur could no longer do much work himself. He invited scientists in various fields to continue the research he had started. Speaking for those fortunate enough to have worked with Pasteur, the biologist Elie Metchnikoff offered a tribute to the spirit of the man and the institute that bore his name:

> *He transferred his enthusiasm and energy to his colleagues. He never discouraged anyone by the air of skepticism so common among scientists who had attained the height of their success. On the contrary, he always kept up their courage and their hope for success. . . . He combined with genius a vibrant soul, a profound goodness of heart, and an extraordinary loftiness of character.*

On December 27, 1892, a special celebration was held in honor of Pasteur's seventieth birthday. Many of the world's most famous scientists, celebrities, and diplomats attended.

The President of France escorted Pasteur down the aisle of the great hall. Joseph Lister, the surgeon from Scotland, gave Pasteur a medal on behalf of the Royal Societies of London and Edinburgh. "There is no one living in the entire world to whom medicine owes so much as it does to you," Lister said. "You have lifted the veil which for centuries has hung over infectious diseases."

Pasteur was so weak, and so overcome with emotion, that he asked his son, Jean-Baptiste, to deliver the message of hope he had written:

Delegates from foreign nations, who have come from so far: you bring the deepest joy that can be felt by a man whose belief it is that Science and Peace will triumph over Ignorance and War, that nations will unite, not to destroy, but to build, and that the future will belong to those who have done the most for suffering humanity.

This was Louis Pasteur's last public appearance. A year and a half later, his health had grown so poor that he could hardly speak. Fearing that he was near death, several researchers from the Pasteur Institute sat with him during the day. Marie Pasteur watched over him at night.

By the end of 1894, though, Pasteur had regained some of his former strength. On New Year's Day, he asked to be taken to the Pasteur Institute. There, he was greeted warmly by younger researchers, many of whom had received their scientific training at his side.

Proudly, they set up a microscope for him. Peering through it, Pasteur saw the germ that Emile Roux and Alexandre Yersin had discovered was the cause of the disease diphtheria. Pasteur sighed, "Ah, what a lot there is still to do." He told friends and family that he wished he had another life to live.

Pasteur's strength slowly faded. That summer, he received many visitors and spent time with his family. Marie read to him from his favorite book, *The Life of St. Vincent de Paul*, about a peasant's son who devoted his life to helping the poor.

On September 28, 1895, Louis Pasteur died at the age of 72. The world mourned the loss of its greatest scientist. In Paris, hundreds of thousands of people lined the streets to pay their last respects to this man who had devoted his life to helping others. Following a service at the Cathedral of Nôtre Dame, Pasteur was buried in a special vault in the Pasteur Institute.

The work of a great scientist contributes to future generations as well as to his or her own. The concepts that Louis Pasteur developed have been the basis for more than a hundred years of discoveries at the Pasteur Institute.

In that time, Pasteur's successors have identified the specific germs that cause typhus, plague, tetanus, and other diseases. They have developed vaccines for such contagious diseases. They have studied the way cancers form and the way the immune system works. They have used science to understand nature and improve human life. Since 1900, eight scientists from the Pasteur Institute have won the Nobel Prize in Physiology and Medicine, the highest honor in the field.

The brick building that once housed the institute is today a 70-bed hospital for infectious diseases. A new complex of modern steel and glass buildings has been built for research work. More than 2,500 scientists and technicians from nearly 60 countries work in 10 departments. The campus at 28 Rue du Docteur Roux is also a teaching center for university students and visiting scientists. In addition to the Paris center, a network of smaller institutes now joins researchers around the world.

The institute's work involves three primary areas: microbiology, developmental biology, and immunology. Microbiology is the study of microbes that cause infections and the development of tests and vaccines to protect people from them. Developmental biology is the study of the way cells form. Research in this area is necessary for understanding genetic diseases, diseases of the nervous system, and the treatment and prevention of cancer. Immunology is the study of the way the body defends itself against disease.

Since Louis Pasteur's time, scientists have learned that the germ that causes rabies is a virus, as are the microbes that cause polio, chicken pox, and even the common cold. The electron microscope, developed in the 1930s, enabled scientists to get their first look at these viruses. In 1991, a department was set up at the Pasteur Institute exclusively to study AIDS (Acquired Immune Deficiency Syndrome), an often fatal disease that affects the immune system. The AIDS epidemic is also caused by a virus.

Scientists from the institute were among the first to identify the specific virus that causes AIDS. They are now experimenting with vaccines to give people protection from the disease.

Most important, the Pasteur Institute maintains the spirit of scientific inquiry that Pasteur valued so highly. In 1988, one hundred years after the institute was founded, its president, Francois Jacob, wrote:

> One hundred years of the Pasteur Institute: all the changes that have occurred in biology and medicine during this century! How can one not wonder what these sciences will become from now to 2088. But there is no chance whatsoever today of providing any answer to this question.
>
> Who would have said in 1850, before the work of Pasteur, that infectious diseases were due to microbes? . . . The most important things cannot, by definition, be predicted. They are the part of our world that some unknown person, in a corner of a cellar or an attic, has the wild idea of changing. Research is unforeseeable. It is up to us to do everything so that the Pasteur Institute, in the future as well as in the past and present, will participate in the great adventure of mankind. Pasteur's contribution to that great adventure has changed the way science looks at disease. His legacy continues to inspire medical research.

Louis Pasteur believed that doing one's best was its own reward. It was the privilege of being human. His own words are perhaps the best summary of his life and work:

> *It does not matter what career you follow. I say to you, do not let yourself be tainted by that spirit of disbelief which likes to belittle everything and will make your work barren. . . . Whether your work succeeds or fails in the test of life, the most important thing of all, as one nears the end, is to be able to say, "I have done what I could."*

For Further Reading

Readers who want to learn more about the life of Louis Pasteur and the history of medicine can turn to a wide variety of materials.

There are several full-length biographies for older readers. *Louis Pasteur: Free Lance of Science*, by Rene J. Dubos (Little, Brown, 1950), offers one of the most complete treatments of his life and work.

There are chapters devoted to Pasteur in several histories of medical discovery. Both *Modern Medical Discoveries*, by Irmengarde Eberle (Crowell, 1968), and *Great Medical Discoveries*, by Ernest Kurt Barth (Random House, 1960), cover Pasteur.

Pasteur's contribution to medicine is covered in several books on the history of vaccination, including *Vaccines and Viruses*, by Nancy Rosenberg and Louis Z. Cooper (Norton, 1971), and *Immunology*, by Martin J. Gutnik (Franklin Watts, 1989). Readers may want to consult *Man Against Germs*, by A. L. Baron (Dutton, 1957), for a history of the fight against disease.

Still entertaining, though somewhat out of date, are two books by Paul de Kruif: *Microbe Hunters* (Harcourt, Brace, 1926) and *The Fight for Life* (Harcourt, Brace, 1926).

Readers interested in the role of women in the history of medicine and health care may want to begin with *Great Women of Medicine*, by Ruth Fox Hume (Random House, 1964).

Index